Little Prayers
THAT WORK

"LET THE CHILDREN COME TO ME; DO NOT HINDER THEM,
FOR TO SUCH BELONGS THE KINGDOM OF GOD."

- MARK, 10:14 NIV

I0157564

CREATED BY:
LARRY S. GLOVER

ILLUSTRATED BY:

HERB WIMBLE IV AND WILLIAM A. RENN, JR.

CHILDLIKE FAITH CHILDREN'S BOOKS

THIS BOOK IS DEDICATED TO ALL OF THE FAMILIES THAT WANT TO HELP THEIR
CHILDREN REMEMBER TO PRAY, BE GRATEFUL, AND TO ALWAYS GIVE THANKS.

MY PRAYER IS THAT CHILDREN ALL OVER THE WORLD WILL LEARN
TO PRAY AND HAVE FAITH FOR ALL THINGS.

CHAPLAIN LARRY S. GLOVER

Published by:
Childlike Faith Children's Books
2012 Wages Way
Jacksonville, FL 32218
childlikefaithchildrensbooks.com

Author: Larry S. Glover
Illustrators: Herb Wimble IV & William A. Renn, Jr.
Editor: Kimberly Benton

Print ISBN: 978-1-7328586-2-6
Ebook ISBN: 978-1-7328586-6-4
Library of Congress Control Number: 2015933762

Printed in the United States of America

10 9 8 7 6 5 4 3 2

Little Prayers
THAT WORK

"COME NOW, AND LET US REASON TOGETHER, SAITH THE LORD"
— ISAIAH 1:18

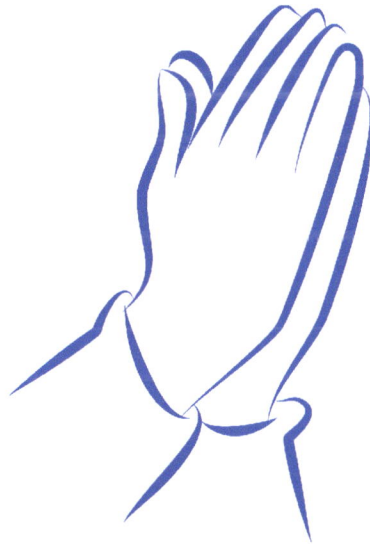

Childlike Faith Children's Books

Dear Lord, I'm praying for my father;

AS HE GOES TO WORK IN THE CAR.
I PRAY HE GETS THERE SAFELY,
AND IT'S NOT VERY FAR.

I PRAY FOR HIM AT WORK;
LORD, HELP HIM WITH HIS JOB.
HELP HIM TO DO HIS VERY BEST;
I HOPE HIS WORK IS NOT SO HARD.

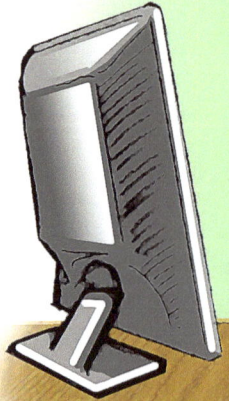

I PRAY WHEN HE COMES HOME AT NIGHT,
THAT EVERYTHING WENT WELL.
AT BEDTIME, BEFORE THE LIGHTS GO OUT,
I LIKE THE STORIES HE TELLS.

DEAR LORD, THANK YOU FOR MY FATHER, AND ALL YOU HELP HIM DO.
I PRAY FOR ALL THE LITTLE ONES BECAUSE THEY LOVE THEIR FATHERS, TOO.

2

Dear Lord, I'm praying for my mother;

SHE HAS A LOT TO DO,
WITH CLEANING HOUSE AND COOKING FOOD,
OH YEAH, AND SOME MOM'S WORK TOO.

WHEN MY MOTHER IS AT THE GROCERY STORE,
I PRAY SHE GETS ALL WE NEED,
SOMETIMES SHE HAS TO GO BACK AND GET SOME MORE
WITH ALL THE MOUTHS TO FEED.

I PRAY THAT AT THE END OF HER DAY
SHE FINDS SOME REST, AND PEACE.
LORD, GIVE HER STRENGTH AND GRACE EACH DAY;
LORD, GIVE HER WHAT SHE NEEDS.

DEAR LORD, I THANK YOU FOR MY MOTHER, THE TIME SHE HAS IS FEW.
I PRAY FOR ALL THE KIDS WITH MOMS, I PRAY FOR ALL THEY DO.

Dear Lord, I'm praying for my sister;

SHE LOVES HER CLOTHES AND SHOES.
SHE'S IN THE BATHROOM ALL DAY; I NEED TO USE IT, TOO.

WHEN MY SISTER WASHES DISHES, SHE DOESN'T TREAT THEM KIND.
I PRAY FOR THE PLATES AND THE CUPS, SHE BREAKS ONE EVERY TIME.

SHE TALKS ON THE PHONE TOO LONG, TELLING HER FRIENDS ABOUT HER DAY.
I WANT HER TO SPEND SOME TIME WITH ME; I MISS HOW WE USE TO PLAY.

DEAR LORD, I THANK YOU FOR MY SISTER
I LOVE HER LIKE YOU DO.
I PRAY FOR ALL THE LITTLE KIDS
THAT HAVE A SISTER, TOO.

Dear Lord, I'm praying for my brother;

HE HAS A PROBLEM WITH HIS ROOM.
HE REALLY NEEDS TO PICK THINGS UP,
AND USE A MOP AND BROOM.

I'M PRAYING FOR MY BROTHER;
HE LOVES THE SPORTS HE PLAYS.
WHEN HE MAKES A GOAL AND HITS A HOME RUN;
LORD, KEEP HIM SAFE ALWAYS.

I'M PRAYING FOR MY BROTHER
AND THE DAYS HE GOES TO SCHOOL.
I PRAY THAT HE PASSES ALL OF HIS TESTS
AND FOLLOWS ALL THE RULES.

DEAR LORD, I THANK YOU FOR MY BROTHER, I LIFT HIM UP TO YOU.
I PRAY FOR ALL THE BOYS AND GIRLS WHO ARE BLESSED WITH BROTHERS, TOO.

Dear Lord, I'm praying for my family;

MY GRANDMA AND GRANDPA, TOO;
MY AUNTS, UNCLES, AND THEIR KIDS,
AND ALL WE GET INTO.

WHEN I VISIT MY GRANDPA AND GRANDMA,
THEY LET ME PLAY ALL DAY.
WHEN IT'S TIME FOR ME TO GO HOME,
I SAY, "OH NO! CAN I PLEASE STAY?"

MY AUNT AND UNCLE LOVE ME,
AND I REALLY LOVE THEM, TOO.
MY UNCLE HUGS AND MY AUNT GIVES KISSES,
BUT PLEASE, LORD, NOT ON THE LIPS.

LORD, THANK YOU FOR MY FAMILY,
AND MAKING US THIS WAY.
BECAUSE OF THE LOVE YOU HAVE FOR US,
I PRAY FOR THEM AND SAY...

DEAR LORD, THANK YOU FOR MY FAMILY, AND ALL THE THINGS WE DO.
PLEASE COVER US WITH YOUR MIGHTY HAND, AND KEEP US CLOSE TO YOU.

Dear Lord, I'm praying for my friends;

THAT I PLAY WITH ALL THE TIME.
SOMETIMES WE FALL DOWN AND GET HURT,
BUT THE DIRT WE DON'T MIND.

WE TAKE A BREAK AND SNACK.
MILK AND COOKIES TASTE SO GREAT.
WE HURRY UP AND EAT ALL OF IT
SO WE CAN PLAY- WE JUST CAN'T WAIT!

AT NOON WE STOP TO TAKE A NAP;
WE PLAY SO MUCH EACH DAY.
IT'S HARD FOR US TO FALL ASLEEP
SO I CLOSE MY EYES AND PRAY.

DEAR LORD, THANK YOU FOR ALL MY LITTLE FRIENDS,
BLESS US IN EVERY WAY.
WATCH OVER US AS WE TAKE OUR NAP SO WHEN WE WAKE UP,
WE CAN GO BACK OUTSIDE, AND PLAY.

Dear Lord, I'm praying for the animals;

AND THEY ARE ALL AROUND.
LORD, KEEP THEM SAFE AND WATCH OVER THEM
IN THE AIR, AND ON THE GROUND.

I PRAY FOR THE ONES THAT ARE IN THE WILD,
AND THE ONES THAT ARE TAME.
I PRAY FOR THE ONES IN THE WATER;
YOU MADE THEM JUST THE SAME.

I'M PRAYING FOR THE LITTLE LAMBS,
AND THE ONES THAT GO "MOO!"
AND I WON'T FORGET ABOUT
THE SPECIAL ONES
AND THOSE THAT LIVE IN THE ZOO.

LORD, I KNOW YOU LOVE THE ANIMALS;
YOU MADE SOME BIG AND SMALL.
YOU MADE SO MANY OF THEM,
AND I KNOW YOU LOVE THEM ALL.

DEAR LORD, THANK YOU FOR THE ANIMALS,
YOU PLACED THEM ALL OVER THE WORLD.
I KNOW YOU TAKE GOOD CARE OF THEM,
LIKE YOU CARE FOR EVERY BOY AND GIRL.

Dear Lord, I'm praying for the world you made;

WE'LL DO OUR BEST TO GIVE.
I PRAY WE TAKE GOOD CARE OF IT,
SO WE ALL HAVE A PLACE TO LIVE.

LORD, REMIND US NOT TO PUT TRASH ON IT,
SO WE KEEP EARTH NICE AND CLEAN.
WE'LL DO THE BEST FOR THIS WHOLE WORLD,
AND FOR THE AIR WE BREATHE.

HELP US LORD TO TAKE CARE OF OUR WATER;
WE USE IT FOR SO MANY THINGS.
LORD, HELP US TO BE MINDFUL
BECAUSE OF THE LIFE WATER BRINGS.

YOU GIVE US EVERYTHING WE NEED
FROM THE GROUND; WE SEE ITS BIRTH.
IT'S ALL FOR US, SO WE CAN LIVE
AND IT ALL COMES FROM THE EARTH.

DEAR LORD, THANK YOU FOR THE WORLD YOU MADE, YOU GAVE US LOTS OF SPACE.
LORD, HELP US TO DO ALL WE CAN TO MAKE EARTH A BETTER PLACE.

Dear Lord, I'm praying for the day you made;

AS THE SUN BOTH RISES AND SHINES.
THE BIRDS ARE SINGING, AND THE FLOWERS ARE BLOOMING;
TODAY IS GOING TO BE JUST FINE!

SOMETIMES, WHEN WE HAVE THOSE RAINY DAYS, I DON'T GO OUTSIDE AT ALL
I SIT AND WATCH YOU WATER THE EARTH, BECAUSE INSIDE I WON'T SLIP AND FALL.

WHEN IT'S TIME FOR THE SUN TO GO DOWN AND SET, IT STARTS TO GET DARK OUTSIDE.
NOW THE EARTH ROLLS AROUND AND BACK AGAIN, SO THE SUN DOESN'T HAVE TO HIDE.

AT NIGHT THE MOON AND STARS COME OUT, ANOTHER DAY HAS COME TO AN END.
IT'S TIME TO GO TO BED NOW, BECAUSE WHEN WE WAKE UP ANOTHER DAY BEGINS.

DEAR LORD, THANK YOU FOR THE DAYS YOU MAKE, EACH ONE IS SO BRAND NEW.
YOU GIVE US LIFE AND AIR TO BREATHE AND I'M THANKFUL FOR THAT, TOO.

Dear Lord, I'm praying for our leaders;

SHOW THEM YOUR AWESOME PLANS.
HELP ALL OF THOSE WHO GUIDE US,
OUR LIVES ARE IN THEIR HANDS.

LORD SPEAK AND WE WILL HEAR YOUR VOICE;
PRAYER HELPS US LISTEN TO YOU.
YOUR LOVE WILL ALWAYS LEAD US,
AS WE KEEP OUR EYES ON YOU.

DEAR LORD, THANK YOU FOR THOSE WHO YOU HAVE PLACED IN CHARGE OF HOW OUR WORLD

I PRAY FOR MILITARY MEN AND WOMEN
WE THANK THEM FOR ALL THEY DO.
I KNOW ANGELS ARE WATCHING OVER THEM
AND OUR LIBERTY AND FREEDOM TOO.

SHOULD REALLY BE. I PRAY THAT IT WORKS FOR EVERYONE AND FOR ALL THE WORLD TO SEE.

Dear Lord, I'm praying
for the people all over the world;

I PRAY FOR GRACE AND PEACE THAT COMES FROM KNOWING YOU, OH LORD.

I PRAY FOR ALL THE CHILDREN, LORD KEEP OUR FAMILIES SAFE,
AND THANK YOU LORD FOR EVERYONE, AND YOUR AMAZING GRACE.

I KNOW YOU LOVE ALL PEOPLE; LORD, HELP THEM KNOW YOU'RE THERE.
I PRAY THAT YOU WATCH OVER THEM, ALL PEOPLE EVERYWHERE.

DEAR LORD, SEE THAT THEY HAVE FOOD TO EAT AND SOME WATER FOR THEM TO DRINK.
I PRAY THAT WHEN THEY LIE DOWN AND SLEEP, WHEREVER THEY ARE,
LORD, GIVE THEM WHAT THEY NEED.

And Dear Lord,

THANK YOU FOR LOVING US
AND HEARING US WHEN WE PRAY.

NOW I'M PRAYING FOR MY FAMILY,
AND THAT WE MAKE IT THROUGH EACH DAY.

AMEN

"TRAIN UP A CHILD IN THE WAY HE SHOULD GO: AND WHEN HE IS OLD, HE WILL NOT DEPART FROM IT."
– PROVERBS 22:6 KJV

Little Prayers
THAT WORK

DEAR LORD,
I AM PRAYING FOR:

_____

_____

_____

_____

_____

_____

_____

_____

_____

_____

THE KIDS EMPOWERMENT SERIES

Order other books by Larry S. Glover:

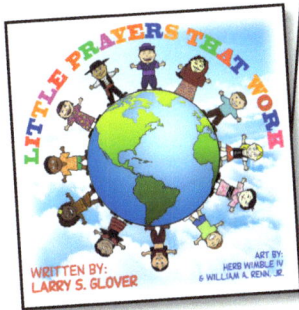

Little Prayers That Work

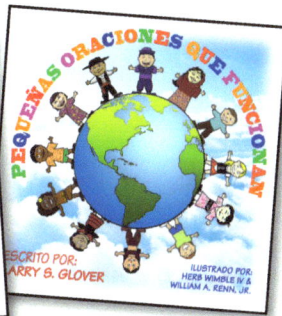

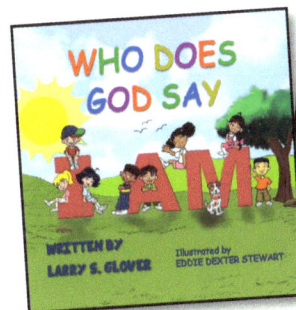

Who Does God Say I Am

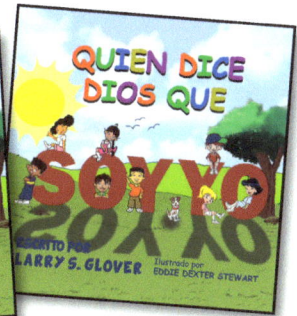

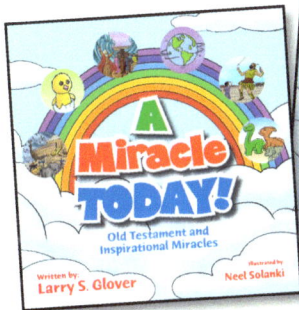

A Miracle Today – Old Testament

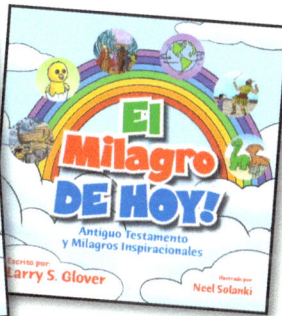

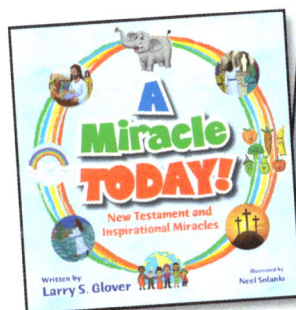

A Miracle Today – New Testament

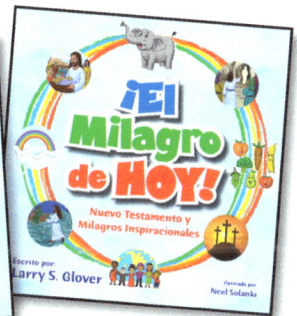

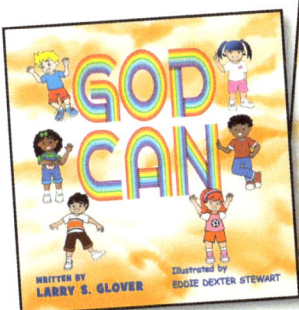

GOD CAN

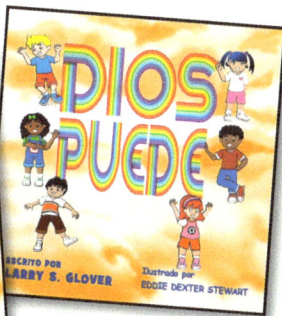

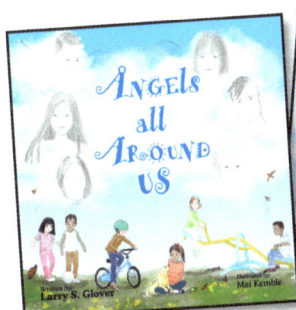

Angels All Around Us

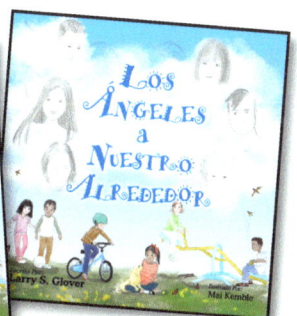

Coming Soon:
A Place Where We Can Go
God is Love

CHILD
LIKE
FAITH
CHILDREN'S BOOKS

Available in English and Spanish
on Amazon.com
www.childlikefaithchildrensbooks.com

THE KID'S VALUE SERIES

Order other books by Larry S. Glover:

Available in English and Spanish.

Be Good

Be Kind

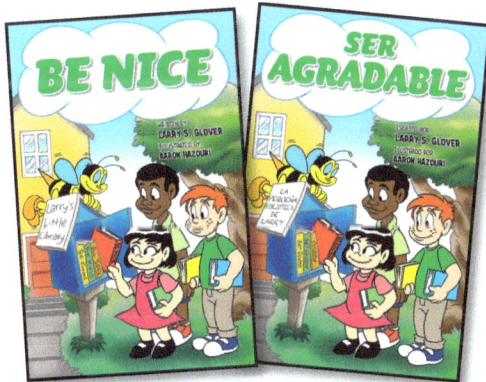

Be Nice

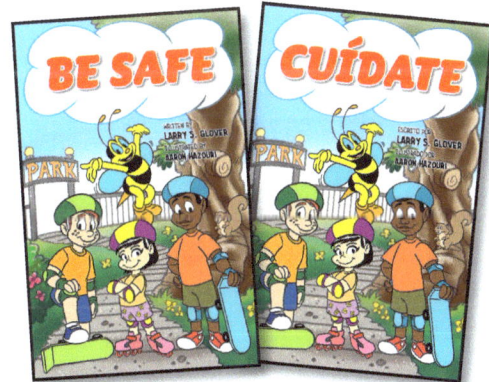

Be Safe

www.childlikefaithchildrensbooks.com

www.ingramcontent.com/pod-product-compliance
Lightning Source LLC
Chambersburg PA
CBHW042107040426
42448CB00002B/169